- 2ND EDITION -

THE JOHN THOMPSON BOOK OF
CHRISTMAS CAROLS

Illustrated by George Williams

ISBN: 978-1-4234-3153-4

EXCLUSIVELY DISTRIBUTED BY

WILLIS MUSIC

HAL•LEONARD®
CORPORATION
7777 W. BLUEMOUND RD. P.O. BOX 13819
MILWAUKEE, WISCONSIN 53213

CONTENTS

Away in a manger, no crib for His bed,
The little Lord Jesus lay down His sweet head;
The stars in the bright sky looked down where He lay,
The little Lord Jesus, asleep in the hay.

The cattle are lowing, the baby awakes,
But little Lord Jesus no crying He makes.
I love Thee, Lord Jesus! Look down from the sky,
And stay by my side until morning is nigh.

Be near me, Lord Jesus; I ask Thee to stay
Close by me forever, and love me, I pray.
Bless all the dear children in Thy tender care,
And take us to heaven, to live with Thee there.

AWAY IN A MANGER

Words by John T. McFarland (v.3)
Music by James R. Murray
Arranged by John Thompson

Deck the hall with boughs of holly,
Fa la la la la, la la la la.
Tis the season to be jolly,
Fa la la la la, la la la la.
Don we now our gay apparel,
Fa la la, la la la, la la la.
Troll the ancient Yuletide carol,
Fa la la la la, la la la la.

See the blazing yule before us,
Fa la la la la, la la la la.
Strike the harp and join the chorus,
Fa la la la la, la la la la.
Follow me in merry measure,
Fa la la, la la la, la la la.
While I tell of Yuletide treasure,
Fa la la la la, la la la la.

Fast away the old year passes,
Fa la la la la, la la la la.
Hail the new, ye lads and lasses,
Fa la la la la, la la la la.
Sing we joyous, all together,
Fa la la, la la la, la la la.
Heedless of the wind and weather,
Fa la la la la, la la la la.

DECK THE HALL

Traditional Welsh Carol
Arranged by John Thompson

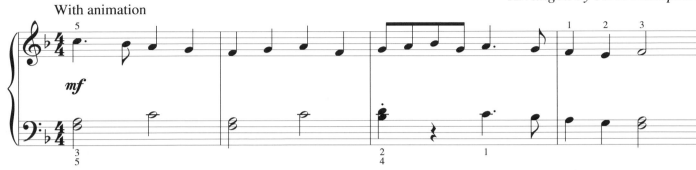

The first Noël, the angel did say,
Was to certain poor shepherds in fields as they lay;
In fields where they lay keeping their sheep,
On a cold winter's night that was so deep.
Noël, Noël, Noël, Noël,
Born is the King of Israel.

They looked up and saw a star
Shining in the East, beyond them far;
And to the earth it gave great light,
And so it continued both day and night.
Noël, Noël, Noël, Noël,
Born is the King of Israel.

And by the light of that same star,
Three wise men came from country far;
To seek for a King was their intent,
And to follow the star wherever it went.
Noël, Noël, Noël, Noël,
Born is the King of Israel.

THE FIRST NOËL

17th Century English Carol
Music from W. Sandys' *Christmas Carols*
Arranged by John Thompson

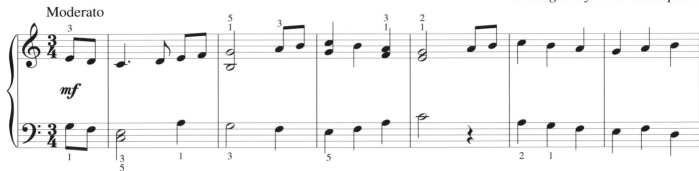

Good King Wenceslas looked out
On the feast of Stephen,
When the snow lay round about,
Deep and crisp and even;
Brightly shone the moon that night,
Though the frost was cruel,
When a poor man came in sight,
Gath'ring winter fuel.

"Hither, page, and stand by me,
If thou know'st it, telling,
Yonder peasant, who is he?
Where and what his dwelling?"
"Sire, he lives a good league hence,
Underneath the mountain;
Right against the forest fence,
By Saint Agnes' fountain."

"Bring me flesh and bring me wine,
Bring me pine logs hither;
Thou and I will see him dine,
When we bear them thither."
Page and monarch, forth they went,
Forth they went together;
Through the rude wind's wild lament
And the bitter weather.

GOOD KING WENCESLAS

Words by John M. Neale
Music from *Piae Cantiones*
Arranged by John Thompson

With animation

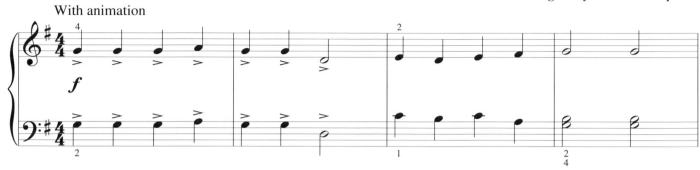

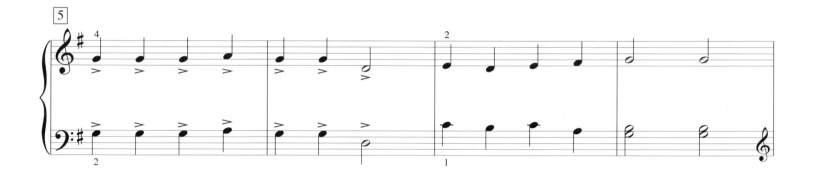

Hark! the herald angels sing,
"Glory to the newborn King!
Peace on earth, and mercy mild,
God and sinners reconciled!"
Joyful, all ye nations, rise,
Join the triumph of the skies;
With th'angelic host proclaim,
"Christ is born in Bethlehem!"
Hark! the herald angels sing,
"Glory to the newborn King!"

Christ, by highest heav'n adored,
Christ the everlasting Lord;
Late in time behold Him come,
Offspring of the virgin womb.
Veiled in flesh, the Godhead see:
Hail, th'incarnate Deity;
Pleased, as man, with men to dwell,
Jesus, our Emmanuel!
Hark! the herald angels sing,
"Glory to the newborn King!"

Hail, the heav'n born Prince of Peace!
Hail, the Son of Righteousness!
Light and life to all He brings,
Ris'n with healing in His wings.
Mild He lays His glory by,
Born that man no more may die,
Born to raise the sons of earth,
Born to give them second birth.
Hark! the herald angels sing,
"Glory to the newborn King!"

HARK! THE HERALD ANGELS SING

Words by Charles Wesley
Music by Felix Mendelssohn-Bartholdy
Arranged by John Thompson

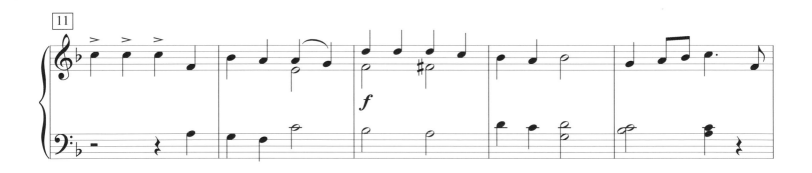

It came upon the midnight clear, that glorious song of old,
From angels bending near the earth to touch their harps of gold:
"Peace on the earth, good will to men, from heav'n's all-gracious King."
The world in solemn stillness lay to hear the angels sing.

Still through the cloven skies they come, with peaceful wings unfurled,
And still their heavenly music floats o'er all the weary world;
Above its sad and lowly plains, they bend on hovering wing.
And ever o'er its Babel sounds the blessed angels sing.

For lo! The days are hastening on, by prophets seen of old,
When with the ever-circling years, shall come the time foretold
When peace shall over all the earth its ancient splendors fling,
And the whole world send back the song which now the angels sing.

IT CAME UPON THE MIDNIGHT CLEAR

Words by Edmund Hamilton Sears
Music by Richard Storrs Willis
Arranged by John Thompson

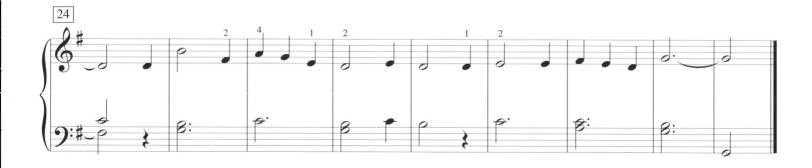

Dashing through the snow, In a one-horse open sleigh,
O'er the fields we go, Laughing all the way.
Bells on bobtail ring, Making spirits bright,
What fun it is to ride and sing a sleighing song tonight! Oh!

Refrain
Jingle bells, Jingle bells, Jingle all the way.
Oh what fun it is to ride in a one-horse open sleigh!
Jingle bells, Jingle bells, Jingle all the way.
Oh what fun it is to ride in a one-horse open sleigh!

JINGLE BELLS

Words and Music by J. Pierpont
Arranged by John Thompson

Jolly old St. Nicholas, lean your ear this way.
Don't you tell a single soul what I'm going to say.
Christmas Eve is coming soon, now, you dear old man,
Whisper what you'll bring to me, tell me if you can.

When the clock is striking twelve, when I'm fast asleep,
Down the chimney broad and black, with your pack you'll creep.
All the stockings you will find hanging in a row.
Mine will be the shortest one, you'll be sure to know.

Johnny wants a pair of skates; Susy wants a sled;
Nellie wants a picture book, yellow, blue and red;
Now I think I'll leave to you what to give the rest.
Choose for me, dear Santa Claus, you will know the best.

JOLLY OLD ST. NICHOLAS

Traditional 19th Century American Carol
Arranged by John Thompson

Gaily

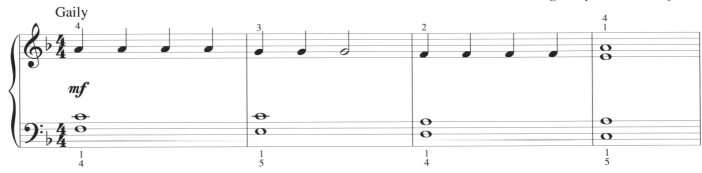

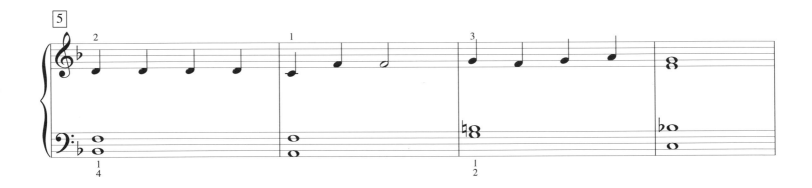

rit.

Joy to the world! The Lord has come; let earth receive her King;
Let ev'ry heart prepare Him room, and heav'n and nature sing,
And heav'n and nature sing,
And heav'n and heav'n and nature sing.

Joy to the world! The Saviour reigns; let men their songs employ;
While fields and floods, rocks, hills and plains,
Repeat the sounding joy, repeat the sounding joy,
Repeat, repeat the sounding joy.

JOY TO THE WORLD

Words by Isaac Watts
Music by George Frideric Handel
Adapted by Lowell Mason
Arranged by John Thompson

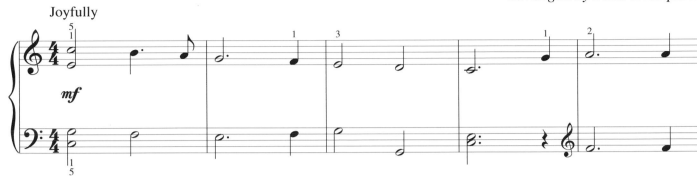

O Christmas tree, O Christmas tree! Thou tree most fair and lovely!

O Christmas tree, O Christmas tree! Thou tree most fair and lovely!

The sight of thee at Christmas tide spreads hope and gladness far and wide.

O Christmas tree, O Christmas tree! Thou tree most fair and lovely.

O Christmas tree, O Christmas tree! Thou hast a wondrous message;

O Christmas tree, O Christmas tree! Thou hast a wondrous message;

Thou dost proclaim the Savior's birth, Good will to men and peace on earth.

O Christmas tree, O Christmas tree! Thou hast a wondrous message.

O CHRISTMAS TREE

Traditional German Carol
Arranged by John Thompson

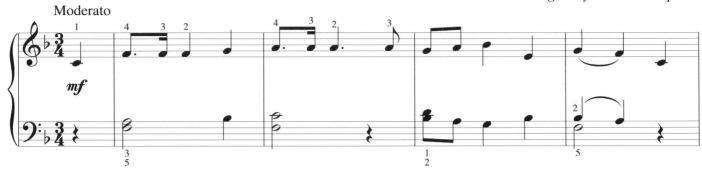

O come, all ye faithful, joyful and triumphant,
O come ye, O come ye to Bethlehem;
Come and behold Him born the King of angels.
O come let us adore Him, O come let us adore Him,
O come let us adore Him, Christ the Lord.

Sing choirs of angels, sing in exultation,
Sing, all ye citizens of heav'n above.
Glory to God in the highest.
O come let us adore Him, O come let us adore Him,
O come let us adore Him, Christ the Lord.

Yea, Lord, we greet Thee, born this happy morning,
Jesus, to Thee be all glory giv'n'.
Word of the Father, now in flesh appearing.
O come let us adore Him, O come let us adore Him,
O come let us adore Him, Christ the Lord.

O COME, ALL YE FAITHFUL

Music by John Francis Wade
Latin Words translated by Frederick Oakeley
Arranged by John Thompson

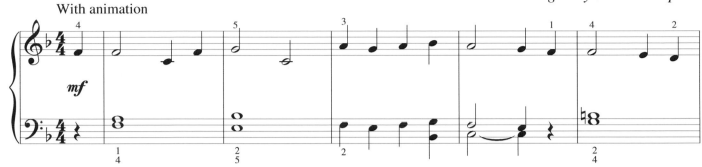

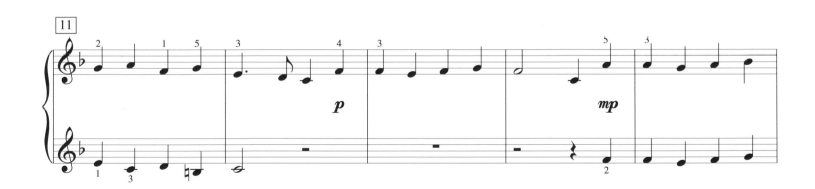

O little town of Bethlehem, How still we see thee lie!
Above thy deep and dreamless sleep the silent stars go by.
Yet in thy dark streets shineth the everlasting light.
The hopes and fears of all the years are met in thee tonight.

For Christ is born of Mary, and gathered all above,
While mortals sleep, the angels keep their watch of wond'ring love.
O morning stars, together proclaim the holy birth!
And praises sing to God the King, and peace to men on earth!

O LITTLE TOWN OF BETHLEHEM

Words by Phillips Brooks
Music by Lewis H. Redner
Arranged by John Thompson

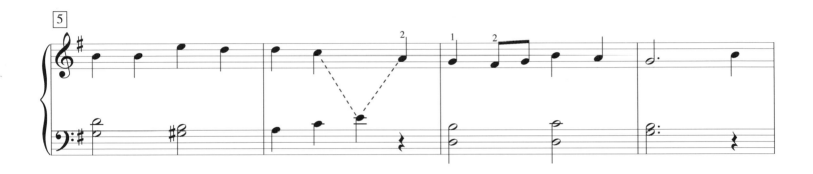

Silent night, holy night! All is calm, all is bright,
Round yon Virgin Mother and Child, Holy Infant so tender and mild,
Sleep in heavenly peace, sleep in heavenly peace.

Silent night, holy night! Shepherds quake at the sight.
Glories stream from heaven afar, Heav'nly hosts sing, "Alleluia,
Christ the Savior is born! Christ, the Savior, is born!"

Silent night, holy night! Son of God, love's pure light.
Radiant beams from Thy holy face, with the dawn of redeeming grace,
Jesus Lord at Thy birth, Jesus Lord at Thy birth.

SILENT NIGHT

Words by Joseph Mohr
Translated by John F. Young
Music by Franz X. Gruber
Arranged by John Thompson

We three kings of Orient are; bearing gifts, we traverse afar,
Field and fountain, moor and mountain, following yonder star.
O star of wonder, star of night, star with royal beauty bright,
Westward leading, still proceeding, guide us to the perfect light.

Born a king on Bethlehem's plain, Gold I bring to crown Him again,
King forever, ceasing never, over us all to reign.
O star of wonder, star of night, star with royal beauty bright,
Westward leading, still proceeding, guide us to the perfect light.

Frankincense to offer have I; incense owns a deity nigh;
Prayer and praising, all men raising, worship Him, God most high.
O star of wonder, star of night, star with royal beauty bright,
Westward leading, still proceeding, guide us to the perfect light.

WE THREE KINGS OF ORIENT ARE

Words and Music by John H. Hopkins, Jr.
Arranged by John Thompson

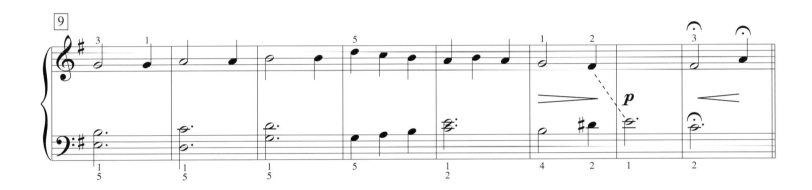

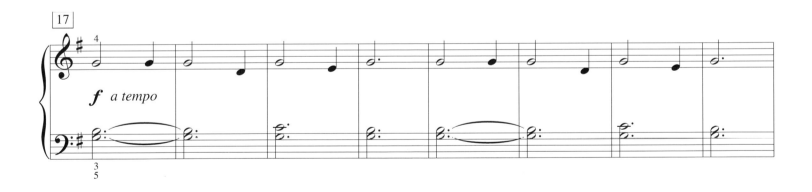